Undone

Sue Goyette

Undone

Sue Goyette

Brick Books

National Library of Canada Cataloguing in Publication

Goyette, Sue
    Undone / Sue Goyette.

Poems.
ISBN 1-894078-33-0

    I. Title.

PS8563.O94U64 2004   C811'.54   C2003-907222-3

We acknowledge the support of the Canada Council for
the Arts, the Government of Canada through the Book
Publishing Industry Development Program (BPIDP),
and the Ontario Arts Council for their support of our
publishing program.

Canada Council   Conseil des Arts
for the Arts   du Canada

Canadä

ONTARIO ARTS COUNCIL
CONSEIL DES ARTS DE L'ONTARIO

The painting on the cover is by
Carol Hoorn Fraser, "Boulevard II"
(1982, watercolour).
For information about the artist
see <www.jottings.ca>.

The photograph of the author is by
Helen Humphreys.

The book is set in Galliard and Janson Text.

Design and layout by Alan Siu.
Printed and bound by Sunville Printco Inc.

Brick Books
431 Boler Road, Box 20081
London, Ontario N6K 4G6

brick.books@sympatico.ca

for Ryan
and
for Robyn

CONTENTS

Forgotten

Kindred

Apprentice

Now she is going to learn
How it is that animals
Can save time:
They sleep a whole season
Of lamentation and snow,
Without bothering to weep.

from "American Wedding"
by James Wright

Forgotten

The Season of Forgiveness

I'm going to lie down next to you
As if nothing has happened
           Charles Simic, "Chorus For One Voice"

In this weather, wood has warped and doors
won't shut the way they should. The mist holds daylight

close, hoarding. When it escapes, the light doesn't
spill, doesn't slide cross the floor, but creeps

and hobbles using furniture to hold itself up. It just wants
to sit. In this weather, light has age, grows rings like a stump

and can no longer hear. It's the ancient relative in the corner
with a change purse and a group of grandchildren at its feet.

Extension wires, 100 watt bulbs, nothing helps. It's faint
and weak and drinks only water. In this weather, not even

the high tide of starlings rolling onto the lawn gets its attention.
"Leave me alone," it says, having forgotten the way it ranted

and raved. How it demanded more time and more flowers.
The garden couldn't keep up, it touched everything:

the silver sugar bowl, the glass fish, every mirror, every drop of water.
And so begins the season of forgiveness, when the birch trees

bordering the yard turn back to bark and branch and you're alone
and I'm alone, the pantry is stocked

and winter is coming up the driveway.

For Women Who Cry When They Drive

Blame it on CBC stereo if anyone asks. Blame it on
the viola. I did and it worked. I never even had to mention locksmiths

and lovers, how close the two are. I never had to name
each white-knuckle grip of his on the steering wheel. I'll name it here, though,

for you. Surrender and all its aliases. I feel at home in two places now.
One's here, the other in the library surrounded by reference books

to the stars. Driving doesn't help. But you already know that. Remember
when you stopped, pulled over on Cole Harbour Road and wept,

bowed to the wheel and the long road ahead, the long road behind. I tried
signalling, pulling over, but the traffic was stubborn. If you are reading this,

I did try to stop. The passing lanes of loss and love and the speed limit
to this life. I held you for days in my heart, dear sad woman in the dark green Volvo

next to the Dairy Queen, next to the Royal Bank, feeling like you have no choice.
And you don't. You don't, except to fasten your seat belt

and yield.

Wife

In the guise of bedtime stories, I might have said
too much. And in the spirit of adventure

I think I've climbed too high. The living room is littered
with books about wizards and surely to god

there is a spell in one of those books for ladders and not just that small,
slender story of the 12-year-old girl and her bottle of immortality:

the pages and pages of choice. I shouldn't let my voice
bulge when I say the word love. They'll grow up

and get it without me. And who needs this headache?
When Ryan was seven, he'd pick vanilla and with the first taste

wail for chocolate. A Baskin-Robbins life lesson. Grass,
I tried explaining, is always greener. But who am I to talk?

Maybe it's contagious the way Caitlin Thomas's life became
a villanelle. The 3rd, the 9th, 15th, 19th: *Rage, dying,*

light.

Back When We'd Try Anything to Fix It

One day, neither of us will be around to explain
the baby bathtub in the attic. It's the only thing up there.
Not even an attic, really, just a space
in the beams between roof and ceiling. We put it up there

on a day like this. Back then, everything was still intact. It was January
and snowing the way it does in Nova Scotia,
foreshadowed and followed by rain. I remember you
saying there is something about the way gulls look

against the snow that speaks of distance,
the blur of white bodies and the lift of their flight,
camouflage of the brief blizzard abandoned
for grey, indifferent sky. I remember trying to figure out

what you meant, what was being foreshadowed
and would follow. Anything spoken with the word
distance in it used to interest me greatly. I thought something
sacred was being said, some celestial message

for me and the direction my life should take. Now I think
you were talking about seagulls, the way their bodies

disappear in snow only to reappear against sky and finally, now,
that's enough. Beauty isn't as hard to reach as I used to think.

It was work, emptying the closet so you could get the ladder in.
We spoke about the clothes we don't wear any more. We spoke
about sweaters. Once in a while the wind would whirl up
and the window would whiten. We both agreed we were glad

to be inside. I remember holding the ladder, watching you disappear,
head first, through the attic opening. I remember thinking it was a type of birth
or rebirth, that something was changing or about to. But I used to
think that way. Life was often just verging on, about to, had to

get better. You kept talking after you disappeared into the attic,
as if the house had found its voice. *Are you sure*, it said, deeply,
forlornly. *Are you sure this will work?*

Jack Gilbert's "Divorce"

Imagine waking up and hearing crying,
that quiet sob of despair and rushing through
the house, then remembering. Looking out

the window to see only moonlight and concrete.
Imagine his hand and his paper, later. He's at his desk,
the whole house behind him, looking over his shoulder,

the door frames, the radiators. Imagine in the middle
of an empty house, the haunting of that quiet despair,
her name like a newly-winged insect searching

for light and some kind of heat, fluttering near his mouth,
the memory of a kiss he still can taste. Imagine
the details of his loss as he shifts through the rubble

of marriage for a poem, something he can manage
to bury again in four lines, bury or somehow illuminate. Imagine him
at his desk choosing where to end the line, after *crying,*

he decides, after *house*. Where else could it have ended?
If he were an architect, he would sketch a small cabin
with high ceilings well suited for the acoustics of the low sounds

of sorrow that waft sometimes like smoke. If he were a teacher
with a grade ten class in front of him, he would try reading
a love sonnet out loud, stopping at the word *true*, his heart groaning

under the weight of it, breaking, a little shift in his chest. He'd conduct
all trains home, make the *soupe du jour* a good chicken noodle to soothe
the tired shoulders of hunched regret, he would only sign out books

with long indexes and black and white photographs and deliver post cards
from tropical islands, throwing the heating bills down the sewer.
He would agree to the construction of a new bridge, cleaning up

the harbour, expanding the city, but he is a poet who sits up in the middle
of the night, thinking he heard her cry. He gets up, looks out
the window and then remembers that she has left and left so hard; the moon,

the concrete coaxing each other out. He sits down at his desk, chooses a pen
and slowly writes *Divorce* at the top of the long blank page of all that is left.

Foundation

It's easy to imagine the surrounding trees,
roots pulled like extension cords, toppling lamps,
light spilling across the floor. It's easy to imagine
the earth being broken, the cement poured,
a foundation, or, the beginning of a house.
We watched the walls rise like water, lapping against the light.

Roots pulled like extension cords, toppling lamps
of poplar, birch light, their leaves small bulbs
of pale green held out in spite of this cold. *Remember me,*
remember me, each bud quivering in the warmth.
It is spring, trees have fallen, there are systems of weather
to forecast. You will not remember me. We will fall.

Light spilling across the floor. It's easy to imagine
windows, wide double doors opening to what is left.
There will be a large expanse, lawn besieged
with weeds. Small, hard strawberries will stay white,
wild. We will mow. The sun will set there, behind that blue house
on the hill. We'll watch it like tourists at first. *Oooh,* we'll say.

The earth being broken, the cement poured,

will be part of the plan. Later we'll try to revise the plan:
we should've taken into account what winter does to it all,
one of us will say. We'll stay up nights trying to remember
who thought of it first. Blame will be the sun right before
it rises, verging, the horizon bulging with it. *You,* I'll say, *I think it was you.*

A foundation, or, the beginning of a house
and everything a house can hold: folded lists of things to do,
that lovely photograph of us all huddled by the Atlantic,
our hair wild, the water about to take us in and the moments after
the photos, after everything to do has been done. Silence, maybe,
or nothing. Nothing. The waves crept onto our feet, the water was cold.

We watched the walls rise like water, lapping against the light
until it was dark. We heard sounds. The house shifting, one of us
would say. How we worshipped the roof when it rained, when it snowed.
We were warm, we were dry, we were lucky, we agreed. O the cost
of a roof. We had no idea. The sun out for a whole season, we'd feel it,
sometimes stood in a slat of it reaching through the walls. *Breathe it in quick,* we'd say.

Neruda's Nets

You knew before you even asked that nets
are sad. They have to be. Isn't that the way

the world works? There are two sides
to everything. We fling ourselves out

in the ocean of our days and drag ourselves
back. Some days we can't even catch

the water. O it's immeasurable, the sadness
of nets. I grieve like a widow, gloved and

alone and married to the thing I bury every day.
Despair, for you are a net sinking and sinking

long past the hour of assault. You've known
the spell that blazes like a lighthouse, you've

gone under, held your breath until your heart
swam into your ears, kicking

and furious. And you know the thing that rescues,
puts its mouth to yours and breathes, is the same thing

that holds you here. Under.

Alone

You stuck one of Ryan's glow-in-the-dark stars
on the closet door. It's been so dark and the star

holds the memory of light, is part of the constellation
of *us*, of *before*, of *remember*. One of the last

stars to appear in our sky. I tuck Robyn in, wait at her door
for her second I love you, call Ryan up from downstairs

then turn out the lights. It's been so dark and now darker.
I lie in bed and think: the cat's out, the wind and the window

are at it again. The ceiling is its own universe, a blank expanse
of sleeplessness. And the star, a guide to the small light

of my loneliness: your closed closet door, the expanse of ceiling
mirrored in the ocean of empty bed. This the darkest voyage,

the ocean swelling, the star so small, every bone of me

awake, hulled, desperate for land.

It's not that I forget
the cat outside. She just wants to stay out
all night. And it's her cry,
plaintive and despairing: *forgotten*, *forgotten*
each morning that wakes me.
And each morning, I open the door
to her joy at finally being remembered.
This is her nature, the nightly melodrama
and relief of morning. If dogs look like
their owners, basset hounded,
beagled, then cats are our hearts:
the purring, the nine lives. The mornings
despairing, plaintive: *forgotten*, *forgotten*.

Can't we both be wind, can't we
both be window? O the long nights
of weather, the wedding procession
of rain and glass and the murmured
disbelief from both sides
of the family. Remember
how we laughed when the dog ran into
the patio door to get at the cat
on the other side? If the dog looks like us
and the cat is our heart, what is the glass
but this marriage, the kids' fingerprints
all over it, the blue sky and clouds
of the other side.

The star is a guide;
the dog resembles.
The cat is always hopeful. It's been
so dark, the bed an ocean,

the ceiling a galaxy
of awake. Darker:

the cat sleeps most of the time;
the dog begs. The bed
cold, each thought a planet
orbiting above it. Darkest:

each planet has its own moons;
each moon its stars. You will stay awake
for many nights charting them
only to finally sleep, wake to the one star
remaining. You will name that star alone,
then get up, let in your heart
but not before it has waited in every corner
of *forgotten*, has seen itself there
on the other side.

Before Mahler's 9th

Each bird is a movement,
the tree a flock of notes,
the slightest wind
sends them.

The light is as irregular as his heart,
listen: small fists of warmth
beating against the window.

A great grief requires stringed instruments.
Only from the tautest tension comes
relief. Rejoice we have no choice but to be pulled
across the long necks of our days, to offer ourselves up
to the music.

On the last day he wrote a coda, dedicated it
to all his sorrow, each note of it a planet with its own
solar system of loss. Planets, moons of loss,

asteroid belts, stars. When he was done, he filled with light,
turned down his supper, chose instead to sit
not on the chair but on the ground. He could feel it,
he said, the steady pulse of earth.

"Where is my coat?" he demanded. "I must walk
if I am to write."

"Forgive me, forgive me" is what he wrote between
the notes. "I have lost sight of all that is good."
His daughter left empty bowls, an empty chair,
a discarded cardigan lying across her empty bed.
He gathers the emptiness in his arms
and carries it with him always.

I imagine all of this in a silent house.
There is a symphony of season
right outside my window.
The leaves are gathering
for their great distance of going
nowhere but under.

I will ask questions
and he will answer them.
I'll research the long corridors
of his heart, look closely
at the photographs he's kept,
and note the scarring, the places
where he's been broken.

"O, he's been broken, I've been broken," his wife says,
picking up his cup and saucer from the piano.
And then she lays herself across the keyboard
and he closes his eyes, raises his hands,
and lowers them, arpeggio.

"Convince me again," he yells to the sunset,
the glorious going down of it, the sky exquisitely left
behind.

The curtains are drawn in the house of his heart.
In each chamber burns a candle and clocks tick

in different directions. He can feel them when he puts his hand
on his chest. He knows it is his breath that will blow out
the flame of himself, he knows it is almost time.

In spite of himself, in spite of November,
in spite of the deep whispered darkness
that has taken to confiding in him, he sings to himself.
"O, wonderful life," he hears himself say.

I am waiting to witness his loss
and already my day has convinced me
that light can conduct anything. Albert the plumber
yells from the bathtub: you must have someone looking
out for you. And the water pours forth gloriously.
The starlings, a great wave of incoming tide
against the window. The herons are right where I think
they are. Waiting.

And After

It wasn't Mahler, the glorious going down
of sun before him and the great need of being
convinced, daily. I don't know that much

about him. Let me speak directly,
let me step from these line breaks and unbutton
the metaphors. Each poem is another way

to say: *convince me*. It wasn't Mahler, it was me. I've spent days
packing up clothes you used to wear when we did groceries, when
Robyn had an earache and we'd take turns walking her

up and down the hallway all night. She has needed a slow, steady movement
always. She complains now at how often I say I'm lonely.
This, she says, *is what you wanted*. Another poem. Another

poem, I think, each time I find myself crying in the Superstore.
Convince me, I ask the columbines, flowering their unpressed
blooms in the public gardens, their buds twisted tight, closed

umbrellas with a far away prediction of flower. *On the Road* is mine.

Truly. I remember buying it. I remember wishing for Jack Kerouac
but you can have him. We're on the road,

we're off the road. We've crossed the dividing line, the passing lane,
the guardrail of our *Friday is movie night*, we're so far from the small
scar of the service road that books won't help. Take them all, all

except Rilke and Neruda. Though poetry doesn't help.
Convince me, convince me in couplets,
in sonnets, in trees, in forests, in plaid shirts with the blue paint

of bedroom on the sleeves. I smelled your clothes as I folded them
and all they smelled of was closet. I wasn't sure if I wanted to smell you,
that mid-eighties St. Zotique, metro smell of you, or if I wanted to smell

me: the love me, love me, love me white corduroy Players Light need
of me. But we were there, the two of us, convincing each other
of forever and family, and O how we believed in every one of the songs

we heard the word love in. It was all for us and it wasn't. Leaving
is the biggest verb I've come across, it's the rock that needs the most
rope, the most muscle to pull up, hoist into the light of day. *Some rocks*

were made to stay under, someone had muttered. Leaving and then
left. Left behind all those days of: *you take him to soccer*
and I'll start supper, the days when we demanded meaning:

what did you mean by that, what do you mean? I still don't know
what you meant when you asked what did I mean. You see the maze
of marriage only from the air but first you have to grow light enough

to leave. You can have all the Audubon. Birds don't convince me
the way they used to. There were whole years of days when I believed
that feathers were a true currency. *Tell me again,* Robyn asks,

about that budgie and the ceiling fan. There is a hunger in us,
I think, for tragedy. I find myself sitting straighter when someone
dies in someone's arms in a movie, I eat my chocolate faster,

thinking: you see, you see, it's all around us. Convince me
October because September didn't come close. The wild asters
were as purple as they could be, I packed up a bedroom full

of *quiet, you'll wake the kids* and found the instruction books
for all the things that need instructions in the top drawer of the dresser
and still hardly anything works. Your leaves will fall,

descend in that whimsical way, mute and lovely and maybe for a moment
they will keep me at the window and we will have a kind of mass together,
the leaves and I, incidentally, O so incidentally, a mass for giving up

and letting go and then the dog will throw up or Robyn will need something
in her urgent way and Ryan in his solitary confinement of adolescence
will bellow and I'll be pulled from the window too soon,

too soon to be convinced. The sky, I wrote, was exquisitely left behind.
I lied. There is nothing exquisite about this.

A Lesson in Tying or Being Undone

There was something about rabbits, one chasing
the other or running around a tree. I could never

remember. Backwards! some books urged, begin
one step behind the bow. The bow, of course, the reward.

Two long loops of shadows, one bowing around
and then under the other. Tied. We were tied together,

you only four maybe five, long laces just wanting
to go. Wait, I'd say, I have things to teach you.

You created complicated systems, laces looped
finally like ears flopped over, the heart of it a knot,

tight and determined to stay together. It was an exchange,
I guess: I taught you to tie, you taught me to undo, patience,

patience following shoe strings around and into, through
the heart of the matter. And what is the heart of the matter?

That our roles have reversed in some way the way
they're bound to? I've taken off my shoes after

the long walk of this and held them up. Undo, undo?
and you, that quiet cry of yours, late into the night,

wanting it to stay tied together, tightly tied, shoes on,
the heart of it complicated, a system flopped over a knot.

Full House

I'm waiting for whatever makes a woman strong
to arrive. This is such a windy August,
that restaurant in Pugwash flattened. And my daughter
has learned poker. Who made the suicide king
so wild? Every day, she takes me to the cleaners, cleans
my clock. Sits at the dining room table with her cards
and a pile of pennies, dealing out hands that make me
fold. *One-eyed Jack*, she says, flipping over
her four of a kind, jack wild. The wind and the hanging flowers:
wild. What is it that makes a woman
strong? Say there's seven levels of sadness
and this is the seventh. Say each step down is more exhausting
than the last and say I've started to watch daytime TV I know
as soon as the announcer nicknames the vulture "wounded
wing" that the bird is doomed. It's the nature
of the nature show. At first his voice is
hopeful, affectionate even, but then he tells us the bird
made a bad choice, commiserates with words like trapped
and final struggle. The bird becomes a mouthful for an alligator,
feet stuck straight out of its mouth like forks, each tine
curled around air and then swallowed. A strong woman

would turn the TV off. Would take a turn at shuffling, see her
five and raise her ten. A strong woman wouldn't have swallowed the bird,
wounded and wrapped around the wishbone
of August. She would've mended the wing, swooped
the bird up and offered it back to the Amazon sky. A strong woman
would never call smiling queens wild, would never have to be told
by her daughter that there are no smiling queens.

A Version of Courage

It's easy to be brave when you're home. Try coming outside,
under the moon, and saying it. There are hollow trees about, tell them about being
done.

If I had to do it again, I'd place a stethoscope on the heart of us
sooner. I'd prescribe Neruda, not the despair but the slow blossom of 20 kisses.

Goodbye, goodbye to the slippery duvet of this bed. The cold floor
of awake and how hope can have insomnia, spend the whole night wishing.

Heartbreak is a geological occurrence. It takes years. Seams, faults
have slowly broken our days apart, their history dates all the way back
to the ocean floor.

Memory is a snare that catches moonlight in its teeth. We've gnawed off
limbs to escape, hobbled to the clearing, each of us with a different story.

Time

The extra hour we all need has its back to us, filling in its blank
agenda book with our names. It lives on the outskirts of this 24-hour town

in a dilapidated wish for more time. If you sneak up to the window
you can watch it, hunched over its kitchen table, eating the kind of meal

you wanted to make with a salad grown in the garden, a linen napkin in its lap.
Its shelves are sagging with the heavy books it's had time to read

and it even took your idea and wrote a fine poem about that boat
at the bottom of the ravine you used to count on when you made your way

to the water. The front hall table has a pile of thank-you notes ready to mail
and postcards inquiring after all those far-flung friends. There is a model

of the mythical ship that carried cures to small islands made of mussel shells
and beach glass. Look how the light moves around it like water splashing

on the far wall. There is something baking, defrosting, slowly rising in a bowl.
The record playing is Spanish Conversation, level one. The Spanish poems

to translate are next to the bed where that extra hour will sleep long enough
to dream of a nightingale landing on its arm like a branch. Don't watch too long.

You'll be surprised how much time you waste wishing for more.

In the centre of all good ideas is a miniature Einstein
jumping up and down, demanding more mystery.

And there's mystery all right, each minute a clue,
a trail that we follow with flashlights and an old version of faith.

There are the kind of minutes spent in a dentist's waiting room,
small, excruciating cavities of time, the long needles of the clock

poised to freeze you there, suspended and worried.
And there are the kind of minutes spent on a porch swing, a heated swarm

of possibilities like fireflies between his lips and yours,
each second a gentle pull closer to the hour when everything

changes. There are minutes spent like pennies and minutes like centuries.
There are gymnastic minutes, double-jointed and executing

a perfect dismount off the beam and right into the heart of the matter.
Then there are isolated minutes with the sweeping light of where you aren't,

the dark minutes without any navigational tools, the slow leak of minutes
and the filling of dread. In some basement laboratory, there are monumental

minutes kept in test tubes for further experiments. The minutes on the moon,
the minute Shakespeare stopped walking to write: *Who's there?* The ghost

of a father minute haunting him from that moment on. It's all relative,
Einstein would say from the rocket-fuelled minute he rode like a stallion.

Giddy-up, he'd say to his time running out.

With the sterling silver tools of regret, excavate the antique handle
at the centre of all time. Call your dead for help and begin to crank

the handle back. Husks of past hours will fall around you the way a tree
leaves itself to the cold. Stop when you're there and step into the moment

like a lake you can't see the bottom of. This is your second chance.
Take the face of your first-born in one of your hands and explain death

again, holding the small goldfish of his youth in the other. The fish
isn't a fish but a small gilled love that your child watched like a clock

winding down. It was overfed and, yes, its bowl was allowed to grow murky,
but in this see the intent, the vast body of water your child swam in,

the small gifts of food he'd catch and carry all the way home for his fish.
Now tell him again, gently, O so gently, how each of his moments is finned

with the same kind of silent, one-sided farewell.

Lilac

I planted it three years ago. Three years ago
I wanted to plant things. I actually planted two.
One died. Frost maybe. I haven't felt like planting

anything for that long. But now I want to see it
flower. All along the sidewalks, there are crowds
of whispering shrubs, the smell of them drizzling

a sweet bruise over evening. Their light
has steeped us all tender and we wander
with no idea of how much we've changed. Abundantly

they flower around me. Abundantly. Except the one
in my yard. That has held out for three years without
flower. Every spring I watch it. The slow convalescence

of a dozen seasons. I'm just glad it made it through
another winter, thankful for the small leaves
shaped like hearts shivering to be outside,

open and so late at night. Three years ago
I planted my heart and then stepped out into the night
without it. I had thought the flowers would be purple;

I've been wrong in so many ways. It had never
occurred to me before to say *flower*. A singular multitude
of blossoms, white and bending over;

the long work it's been just to open.

Kindred

His Green Age

The boat in the ravine begs for a story. When the wind settles,
roosts in the gangly pines, the lake is so close

it can taste it. A plain rowboat, the pale blue
of the edge of sky on what promises to be

a hot, clear day. It's a cradle now for all the dead
leaves that have found their way afloat. So close,

so far from water that it's barely what it is but has become
a marker on the trail. About to, its prow points, starboard

to the road, port to the wild raspberries, it's so thirsty
it's curling up at the sides. Let me tell you of the man

who built it. It was the summer he was reading
Dylan Thomas, trying to memorize the words

Thomas used the most. He'd sand the long side of it,
reciting: *I sea man, love like sun.* There was a longing

in him, his heart an oar that dipped and pulled to a shore
he could only imagine. *As time lie night*, he was alone:

wind water light and the boat answered a need, gave his hands
a place to rest. *Sleep over, green.* He'd lie awake

and still feel its hull like a *moon*, the swell of *house* under *sky*, the quiet *turn*
of her *ghost*, and then he'd dream the long dream of *grave*, of *star* and *tree*.

It was a summer of mourning, the dirt road and its puddles reflecting
the *white world* of emptiness. He missed her;

stone tongue. Wound. And would try to hear her
in the sawing of cicada, see her in the meadow, swollen with milkweed

and chicory. *Sing tell, still summer* the boat took shape
beneath him. He had no plan, no *walk*, no *word*, no *seed*

that drove him forward. He built his boat, he carved its oars
and was stilled only by the *weather*, its *voice*, each raindrop of the *year*,

a decade of days. His *lover*, his *lover*, the slow, sad slide down into bramble.

A Late Horizon

for John Thompson

He wrote the word *emptiness* on the back of a poem,
but first he wrote of tables and of listening, both set for a meal.
Some heartbreaks are shotgun, instant, and fall over something small.
Get up now from that kitchen chair of despair. Bring back the empties.

But first he wrote of tables and listening, both set for a meal,
and then he set steel traps along his loneliness, hoping to catch its heart.
Get up now from that kitchen chair of despair. Bring back the empties.
What you find in the morning, you skin and feed off of all winter.

And then he set steel traps along his loneliness hoping to catch its heart.
He followed its footprints deep into the woods, his breath caught and scared.
What you find in the morning, you skin and feed off of all winter.
The memory of you is part bullet, he said to his table, to his bed.

He followed its footprints deep into the woods, his breath caught and scared.
It takes courage and an anvil heart to stay under the moon and speak like this.
The memory of you is part bullet, he said to his table, to his bed,

your love a marsh of high grass I got lost in.

It takes courage and an anvil heart to stay under the moon and speak like this.
The weight of it makes his legs buckle. Don't look now as he falls.
Your love, a marsh of high grass I got lost in,
each step away from the house was a voice that said: *don't.*

The weight of it makes his legs buckle. Don't look now as he falls.
After he's gone, see how the grass is still crushed, the earth cupped to hold him.
Each step away from the house was a voice that said: *don't*
and he did. Each step necessary in his constellation of trail. Each step hunted.

After he's gone, see how the grass is still crushed, the earth cupped to hold him.
The scorch of desire, the greater-than signs of geese leaving
and he did. Each step necessary in his constellation of trail. Each step hunted.
There is a late horizon here and a whole season, the trigger is cocked. Take aim. Fire.

The Beginning of Avon

Long before power bills and Girl Guides selling cookies,
there were men armed with heavy books of Shakespeare

knocking at doors with a mission. *Time and the hour runs through
the roughest day.* It was their job. To sell. *My lips, two blushing pilgrims,*

ready stand to smooth that rough touch with a tender kiss. How their feet
must have ached, the roads winding and hard, those books heavy,

heavy with guilt, with betrayal, with haunting. *Had he not resembled my father
as he slept, I had done't.* Weary, they were, knocking on the wooden doors

of their time. And the ladies of the house answering to each Shakespearean
O: *O, that she were an open et caetera, O me! what eyes hath Love*

put in my head. Those Os had their own climate, their own pulse.
They pursued the women answering the doors and convinced them

by lingering on their lips to buy. *O, swear not by the moon,
the inconstant moon.* And if they bought a volume, they'd receive,

free of charge, a bottle of perfume, the men coaxed, part of the deal. Perfume
to daub between breasts, perfume to lure more Os

into their lives. The women bought Shakespeare like hot cakes,
not for his tragedy, not for his grief — they knew all about that — they bought him

for the perfume. *Hot thoughts beget hot deeds, and hot deeds is love.* Perfume
was lighter fluid for the heart, and they ached, how we've always ached,

for more Os.

Here Lies the Water and Here Stands the Man

Poor Miss Ellen Terry climbed into bed to memorize
her lines. *Is it possible a young maid's wits should be as mortal*
as an old man's life? She woke up as Ophelia and spent the day

in bed. I know nothing about her except what I see in the photograph,
holding what? Rosemary for remembrance, pansies for each thought?
In the weeks before opening night, she'd lower herself

into her bath, slowly, as if for the last time, the rushing water,
the stream that frothed around stones, the embankment too slippery
to climb back up. *To have seen what I have seen*, she'd whisper, *see*

what I see, and then she'd go under. She began to lose her appetite,
invent small songs her voice trickled through, tears seven times salt.
And will he not come again? she'd ask. It was spring, she began to believe

what she was saying, the watchman of her heart wringing its hands:
be careful my bonny sweet Ellen. But she shooed warnings away like flies.
Her loneliness now coloured a new pale green that beckoned her

to sink to her knees in. O, she played the part madly,
lying there, Ophelia acting dead, her brother, a requiem standing over her,
forty thousand brothers worth of rue. And when she finally got up,

the woman will be out, adieu, she'd leave her there, a strange
empty Ellen, a living monument, holding the earth off awhile longer,
stepping gently from the flat mountain into the long sixth act of stage.

Kindred

Snoopy hunched over his typewriter:
It was a dark and stormy night. Every one
of his novels started with that line. He knew

how to live, dancing, abandoned,
head back, his feet a blur, a whirr of joy. He knew
we all have our own beginnings and they're all the same.

He ran away from home, he howled
at the moon, his little beagle body full of dark,
of storms. He knew when he was hungry.

His best friend was a bird. The more I think
about him, the more I like him. He wrote
in the rain, his black dot eyes intent,

intent on his page.

Movie

story

Forget about the light, tell me the story,
tell me about the young girl's heart asking:

are we there yet, are we there yet? And tell me about her mother
whose heart never left home, who watched the world

through a window smudged with dog snout and her answer:
No, she'd say. *No.* Tell me, does she ever get there,

the young girl? Does she ever arrive? And what difference
does sunlight or moonlight make, the cedars lit like lanterns,

the hyacinth and its leaves, pale green paper. Every night
that girl must write in the small diary she keeps in her sock drawer,

the key hidden between pages 30 and 31 of the *How and Why Wonder Book
of Time. How to check your watch by the stars: if your watch is accurate,*

the star will disappear 3 minutes and 56 seconds sooner than the previous night.
Streetlights have nothing to do with it. Tell me she doesn't become

a star, disappearing earlier and earlier every night. If loss radiates
its own kind of light then so must she. Think of lamp shades,

think of me and how you say I shine, my skin awake to your touch.
Isn't that our job? To coax out the light in the story, to say, finally,

that she doesn't disappear earlier and earlier every night.
If she is part star then she returns sooner, her heart

beating a small light against a whole skyful of dark.

light

The light is the story. It's part plot
and part mercury, breaking into puddles of yellow lamplight

that set like wax holding the mother in her place. And she stays there,
an unlit wick, watching each possibility drive by her house.

See how her yearning shines off those cars, slivers of sunlight
gash her like glass. Light is the true narrator, it documents

her loss. The script is just hurdles, trees it has to bend around
or fall through. The young girl reflects it the best. Watch her

let it move through her. She gives over to it and that is pure story.
Of course she's part star and she disappears, but in disappearing

reappears. Next time you're in the kitchen in the dark, think of her
and stay there. Soon the toaster comes out, the kettle,

the long curve of tap, dials and the spoons from our tea. Stars.
I hardly hear you when I'm touching you, moth soft and porch light.

She'll always be drawn to it. Her story is just how close she can get.

For the Poem I Read On October 24th

I've lost you and you're everywhere. Were you in couplets

with the word *time* implied between each stanza
or did I just imagine it? The heart of you was a woman

sitting on the front porch, the steady beat of her listening.
Love, she called out, *oh*, *this loneliness.* Okay, she didn't really

call that out. She thought about balancing
and about her life, about his wife. It was fall, the leaves

moved the way birds do in Disney movies, happy endings
fluttering from the sky. She had long hair and was sure

of herself. I've looked through all my books for her,
for the house she sat outside of, for him putting down

the dish towel and coming out to her, sitting by her.
There you are, he'd say, *I've missed you.* Maybe you were
in tercets, the two of you having a fight over something

he said. Maybe it wasn't his wife washing or wiping the counter,
maybe it was his sister, or your sister or a friend. *What is it
that I've lost? Oh, this loneliness.* Do you see what happens

when you lose something? The nature of loss is everywhere
it isn't. *Go where you had it last*, my mother would say. A house,

a front porch. *Forget about it*, she'd say, *then it will turn up.* Tell me
he didn't turn off the porch light and close the front door. Tell me

you're still not out there, sitting on the patio chair, waiting.

A New Form

Multiply the time of your birth with the year
your house was built. Now stretch out your arms

and measure the length from the tip of your right index finger
to your left ring finger and add that to the weight of your first true

sorrow, the first time something actually stopped you
in your tracks and dismantled you. This is when you might

want to hire someone to help with the research: go out into the field
and count the population of the nomadic letter s. It's

everywhere, wreaking havoc and making even the smallest
of mistakes plural. Now add to that the number of wine bottles

you've uncorked, thinking that pouring wine should be a type
of ceremony, a threshold to the countless possibilities of passion. Then subtract

the number of footsteps it takes to walk the territory the mockingbird
so ferociously guards in your neighbourhood; ignore his impersonation

of a burglar alarm, his menacing cat noise, his clothesline pulley. He's just a bird cursed with tail feathers that look like the last two petals

of a plucked daisy, he loves me, and O, as he flies away, he loves me
not. Now you should have one big number on your hands.

Write it down somewhere, on next year's calendar maybe,
on the day the clocks spring forward or if you're feeling even the slightest bit

melancholy, on the day the clocks fall back. I think we might've been barking
up the wrong tree. Numbers may be the true metaphor. Try this little test:

think of a number between one and ten then figure out
what that number represents, how it's significant to you.

Maybe it's the number of people you have really opened up to
in bed, or the number of times you truly regret not saying yes,

or the times you were caught straddling a window, escaping
or sneaking in. Isn't it strange, eerie how it works out? Coincidence?

I think not. The big number you've written down is either how many breaths
you've already breathed, the number of kilometres left for your feet

to walk or the weight in ounces of your next real joy. That part of the formula is still foggy. I went to the sacred well and drank the deep water

of the Otherworld, I ate salmon, rowan berries, hazelnuts and danced
around a fire for several days. Apparently I spoke in tongues and left drawings

of the square root of my spirit on several of the village walls.
I took a young sparrow from its nest and fed it slivered almonds for forty days

then carried it back to the meadow and recited the geometrical formula
for the angles of white light that move through birds before releasing

them to the longitude of blue, latitude of sky. Sure, I left it
with a few treasured words by Rumi, but I couldn't help myself.

Flight and ecstasy always seem to go hand in hand. I even bought
and read the easy how-to book they were selling on the last day

of the workshop, I went to the readings and heard masters recite
the height of their huts multiplied by the cubic weight of their unrequited

love added to the 243 earth days that make up one day
on the planet Venus, but I'm new at this and, to be honest,

I'm still not sure I really get it.

Meadow

St. Peter's

A tree is a love letter, a tall pine,
slender and unopened, waiting
to be read. It is whisper, it's all ears
and it's moonlight
dressed up in wood
and needles and cloud. Roads stretch
all the way to morning
or all the way to night. All of darkness
may be behind you or just ahead,
all of light.
And this footbridge, small and necessary,
is a hand reaching back, a lover
on her way home from his house, the placing of each plank,
her desire.
And the meadow is mirror and nest. The genealogy
of grass. Distant cousins. Great-great-aunts. I am
surrounded. Beneath, above, they all move

through me and I lie on this bridge, each plank
a vow, each bird a wish, and I respond leaf
to leaf: *yes, I am yours* and *yes,*
yes, you are mine.

So Quite New

(after e. e. cummings)

The leaves are excruciating. So small and feathered. A limb
of green ache limbering up
for the rest of the season. And in each
a heart whose fatal song
hums along because how can it know
the words? Here's to opening
and upward and the way my muscles
muscle and to the flesh that holds all of you
together. Unbearably, it's spring and I must confess
that I've spent summers watching satellites
thinking they were stars and who knows what it is
you are.

Kiss

There has to be a small seed of amnesia
in every kiss or we'd remember

how there's a small seed of ending
in every beginning. In the language

of deciduous, green means again
and again is a word that must be

repeated. Like a kiss
because we forget everything: the dark

channel of water our hearts have swum
to be here, the small boated nights we leaned

from, our hope barely afloat,
the thin branches divining loss. We forget the pale

path of moonlight we clung to like a railing.
We kiss and the trees in the streetlight are green.

The winter, the worst we've had for years,
is behind us. Maples maybe, or oak, each leaf

a whisper *again and again*, each kiss a wish *remember
and then forget*.

Psychic

To the man, stooped with age, who took a century
of small steps to the miniature coffin of the saint:
I only have this chair to give. I know it's simple,
but it's made from the wood of the tree that once
offered shade to the first and only woman you loved
and she accepted it, gratefully. The sun was always so warm
when she loved you, all the clouds had migrated from those years,
to the east of lonely. She wants me to tell you it's the moon,
the thin hook of crescent that has trapped her
beneath the river. She wants me to tell you
she's waiting, holding her breath, and can feel the beginning
of fins where she'd always imagined she'd have wings.

To the young man standing in the driveway with the suitcase
and fishing rod, facing the house and waiting: Don't.

Carry those heavy coins of silence and exchange them
for paper to write the letters of forgiveness you've got stored
in your heart. The currency of your words, the hand that writes them,
will afford you a piece of land overlooking water. Every morning
you'll be able to watch the shy offspring of memory drink while you write
your way back home. He wants to tell you
he can't imagine the husk of a word being able to hold
everything he wants to tell you. He wishes he had more time,
had started earlier, planted the seed of each thought.
By now he'd have trees to give you. As a father should,
he wants to add, as a father should.

To the woman who is asking about her brown-eyed child:
the answer is yes.

To the person wearing a borrowed coat:
someone is urging you to finally speak the truth about being cold.

The spirit of a praying mantis would like an audience
with all teenage girls. It wants to tell them they both share
the long-limbed green hope of melting into leaves
and the same aphid hunger to be noticed, the same wanting
to be gently held, exclaimed over and then returned
to the camouflage of the many.

The trees want us to know they're not as sad
as we think, that they may look solemn
with their pillared trunks but they're part of an ancient ceremony
and are the true threshold of twilight.
And though we aren't the precious gem of bird,

the jewelled flock clasped against the sky,
we are revered for our skill in praising them.
Emily Carr, they want us to know, is an honorary
member of the forest, like that amateur photographer
who caught the grove of birch in the sombre light
that predicted his death. The photograph hangs
over his bed now as if it rose from his body and lingered there:
his last pure thought, framed.

A new language is coming, pushing its green self through
the sidewalk squares of our tired talk. The red huckleberry
is in charge of conjugating the word *thirst*, assisted by the yellow violet.
Thoreau, they insist, is the new verb, Chanticleer the royal noun.
Our children will be taught the shifting hieroglyphics
of flock, will have copybooks and a special pencil
for marking down the measurement of rain. They will recite their forests,
tree by tree, and will be quizzed, multiple choice,
match each bird to its feathers. We will stop fighting
and surrender, finally paint the walls of these houses

the colour they should be. There will be a family reunion
in the southwest meadow, bouquets of new dictionaries for everyone.

If you were born at midnight: turn your watch back
one hour. Take sixty minutes to reword what you want to say,
less one minute for the small ceremony of thanks
for the question mark. It is the fork in your road. Answer yes
and you will be led to water. No and you will be left alone
with two chairs and a long evening. Either way, you have 30 minutes left
to say what you really mean.

Your mother wants you to know that when she said You can't,
she meant you can. When she said Don't be late, she meant
Stop at the edge of the road and watch how darkness is part creek,
sloshing at its own banks. Knowing how the darkness starts

will later somehow help you more than anything I can say.

For the one woman who is still holding out hope
that Elvis is still alive: He isn't. He's no longer the king
but the concierge at Heartbreak Hotel, and he's expecting you.

There is a man who wants me to tell his wife
he's sorry he left first. It was unexpected
and he wants her to know that the park bench
is still there with their initials carved on its back.
Heaven, she had called it back then, and it was.

The future wants me to tell you all that it doesn't
want us. Instead of waiting for it, peering down
the empty track of arrival, we should just stay
where we are and try to keep busy. It wants me to say that it makes its fortune
by not ever really turning up and it's not about to
now. It's grateful for the predictions we make
but, really, it likes being elusive, running ahead, out of
touch, so stop chasing it, it didn't do it, it has a whole history
of alibis, you can't ever blame it. Its role in the holy trinity
of time is to be after, always. Worship it
with a ceremony that involves water and three stones. Stay up as late
as you can with your bowls of sunk rocks then say a small prayer
of surrender and point overhead to the passing day. The future is the flexed muscle
of faith and has trained for the marathon. Our place is in the middle
of the two eternities with our walking sticks,
our slow pace, our stories.

Homage

There is a whole school of fish, low in the ocean,
swimming in the formation of Jacques Cousteau's

last words. Mona, Mona in your Moulin Rouge
heaven, strip off those doubts draped across your chest

and show us your hurting heart. The dead go on talking with their long
tongues and slow words. The trees quake from being climbed

quickly, haunted by the young poet shimmying up their trunks
to whistle nightingale for the world. And all the pet goldfish

are left to spend eternity swimming, swimming towards what
feels like ocean. North of the ear is where secrets are clutched,

and if that phrenological map were wrapped around the globe
we'd see how forests are the planet's true ears. This is the year of the horse,

the first month being "Muzzle." Aren't we all holding our hands,
coaxing out time with a desperate sugar cube? The barber gave away

the king's secret to the willow tree, the willow tree gave away its wood
to the harp and the harp could only play what was true. Our dead play

hosanna deep into the night and we dream we are children
who have rescued a wounded gull from the Atlantic.

We've set its wing, reminded it how to fly and in return
it has told us navigational secrets, the magnetic force

of longing and the expanse of love that is sometimes mistaken
for ocean. O, it talks down the sky for us and we're languid in cloud,

not wanting ever to wake up. These are tight times, hind-quartered
and dark, and we're riding wild, bareback, the branches low, our saddlebags

empty of mail. If the juncos held string in their beaks,
the backyards would be parcelled and ready to send by now. *Handle with care*,

the dead have always written with their invisible ink. *Fragile.*
Then they deliver us back to ourselves in slow blooming seasons.

Hosanna. They've given up their hearts so we can hear
music plucked from the trees. They touch us lightly, stroke our temples

when we sleep and fix the wounded wings of our secrets. In return
we whisper our pledge to the next generation, our children

and their children swimming free from our nets. We leave offerings,
small nests, tufted soft with memory and every time we speak the names

of our dead, one of them chooses between dorsal fin or plume.
Beatrice, Florence, Jonah, Lawrence. It will take all of our breath,

every bit of willow wood to name them truly. *Eva, Elizabeth,*
Martin, Sam. The sky darkens with new birds, the ocean

phosphoresces with new fish.

Issa

The poet Issa took an hour from nursing
his dying father to walk. Each step a syllable
in the long letter home. Give the man a cart full
of roofs and a young wife and dare him

to be happy. The dying have a thirst and thirst
is always the first lesson and the last. There is a field of grief
to plow, the sun long to set and still he is puzzled
by the wrong weather. To quench him now would be

like pick-pocketing the poetry right out of him.
The tired lean of Issa in the wind. Courage
and cold water won't even come close. The night
is a hot forehead; the stars, spoonfuls

of boiled medicine. The cats have their fleas,
the flies their bowls, and Issa has his moments
he worships in like a temple. His heart, the small clay cup
he holds to his father's dry lips. Drink. The well outside

is filled with rain. What is it to crave without quench?
What is it to move in the world without a mother,
to go on teaching of the great ocean beneath all that is said?
The bell longs for its mountain and the mountain,

as the ringing dies down, turns to its bell, reminding it in small kisses
of what it was, faint echoes of the same farewell. Issa sits
with the helpless trembling of memory to write: *the twentieth-night moon
shone in*. Devotion recollected in slow snail steps

and a death poem under the pillow, a note of short breaths
explaining everything. The moon had urged him, the moon
sweet-talked him into stealing off with all the plum blossoms,
an armful of his youth wilting in his hands. Issa, poet of the seventh day

of the seventh month coming apart, as all that meets will part,
even now under his glorious, unexpected, asway, aswinging sky.

On Hearing Elizabeth Bishop Read Her "Crusoe in England"

Her voice is a blouse, crushed berries one
by one and then hours apart, open. Each word an island
with one kind of everything. O, I'm transported;

the archipelago of poem, her voice the bright blue
violet that creeps over everything, the ocean
of time around us, tide high and then retreating:

all the hemisphere's left-over loss at once. Was there
a moment when I actually chose this? Ten miles away,
a memory was being born and she swerved from its shore,

Mont d'Espoir; my despair, and navigated around the sinking
ship of family, the dreams of food and love. None of the books
have ever got it right. Her voice rained so much,

she built shelters of elegy around herself, invented umbrellas,
parasols. How, she wondered, could anyone want such things?
There were years, fifty-two miserable weeks in each, small volcanoes

she climbed thinking of caves, the faint glimmer of sky,

the way out. She'd been dyed early with bright red berries,
pale, pale Elizabeth, and then her mother didn't even know her.

When the birds leave her voice, all at once, the sound
is of a big tree in a strong wind. And other times, her voice
is a knife, begged, implored not to break. Every nick,

every scratch a cicatrice where once were leaves.
Her voice is a lantern, a spiked walking stick for climbing
over herself, it's a crucifix. It lives and, even now, delivers

the gossip, whispers the gospel, testimony of the long dead
according to the first chapter in the book of being stranded on a poem.

Her Bangs

She spends most of her time fixing them. They curl
up, flip, won't stay the way she wants them to.

Only a few years ago, when she was six,
she'd look hard at me thinking purple with all her might

until I shook my head in wonder. She thought she could
change the colour of her eyes. What's your secret?

I'd ask. Just think purple, she'd answer breezily, and *ta da*,
your eyes are purple. Remember how you used to turn your eyes

purple, I ask her now at breakfast, her bangs wet and curlered.
She just shrugs and picks the marshmallows from her bowl

of Lucky Charms. Lately she's been screaming because spiders
make it past all of our feet, past the cat and into her room to swing

and sway from their webs. I give a pretty good talk on spiders now,
the ratio of their size to hers, their worth to the planet. I recite a haiku

about keeping a careless house. And I can talk about curls,
how they soften a face, the liveliness of them. She's ten

and understands pig Latin, though it took her awhile
to unscramble the *onkey-may it-shay* her brother called her last night.

She's not indignant until morning, fishing out blue moons,
pink hearts from her bowl after a long night of figuring it out.

It's all so delicately balanced, I say to her bent head,
bangs stiff with gel, your brother who you say you *ate-hay*

rescues you almost daily from spiders, stands on chairs to catch
and then carry them cupped in his hands outside.

The hair that escapes her ponytail corkscrews
question marks at the nape of her neck. An abundance

of luck floats in her bowl, four-leaf clovers, pots of gold.
At six, she knew the secret. *Ta da* she said to me,

her voice slender and sure as morning sunlight
reaching the table between us, and it was that easy: purple.

Tattoo

Last night, Robyn stood in line
for a turn on the Gravitron. I watched her

from the car. It was raining. She got on,
strapped herself in and waited for the force

to press her against the wall.
Amusement Parks. Fairs. I sat in my car,

its own kind of Gravitron, and felt each of your words
spin their vortex, my heart pressed hard

against its wall.

Take any kind of stone, smooth and flat stone
for skimming, fool's gold, the stone out

of your shoe. Let's call it truth.
The stone of truth. Find water and drop the stone

in. See the truth ripple in every
direction. See how memory alters and predictions

shift. See how you sink to the bottom and are left
looking up through water at the sky.

O'Keeffe stayed in the room with her irises
for the two weeks they lived, not wanting to miss

a moment of their movement. I saw you the same way,
saw you open and bend. Were you the two weeks

that held the mystery or were you the iris,

the slow giving over, the sliding down, the crumple

of flower? Throw that stone into this water,
what ripples is the purple leaving, the florist

reluctantly wrapping the flowers, selling them
and then watching them go. The same florist

later at home trying to find the right words to tell
his lover the purple of them, the way the petals give

like her legs and arms. And the stone is the quick dream
of Georgia that leaned down from a femured moon

and whispered: "the pelvis of lilies, the petal of bones."
The stone is the empty glass that still holds water,

that special, aged water of iris that, if swallowed,
would taste of you coming and then going. The stone is the truth

of my thirst settling deep.

The florist's lover left awake puts her lips
to his fingers and licks them, tasting flower,

and Georgia O'Keeffe stirs in her bed, passion
pacing the cage of ribs that holds it, snarling to get out.

Your love is water for a cut stalk, the florist wants to hear, even in his sleep.
Georgia wants purple like there's no tomorrow.

And what do I want? I want the man about to tattoo me
to think of light and love with every needle.

His eyes wrung-out sky and water, the stone
of pupil sunk in their centres looking at the small of my back,

truth rippling the way it does, out from him and lapping up
on all the shores, the curved land, the faint outline of where your hand
has been.

It's just a symbol for light, the tattoo. And the Gravitron
is just a ride. Georgia O'Keeffe said she only painted

the holes in pelvic bones because, as a child, she liked to eat
around the hole of a donut, the raisin in a cookie.

The truth is always pressed hard against the heart,
and in the hollow of bones. O'Keeffe got close,

as close as she could. Imagine her bending over an iris,
briefly and for all of time, before breathing in, tasting

the space around the flower, swallowing the vortex
that spins and sinks it deeper, from bulb to bud to

blossom. She swallowed the truth of it whole and then stood up to it,
turning herself into the water it needed to reach the shore

of its canvas, or the stone of its poem.

Apprentice

Apprentice

One long ago twilight, the *duello* between longing
and having was carved on the secret wing of the great migration

of light. Now, every night as it flies over dark water, light recites
the agreement: the dropping of gloves, the number of paces

before turning and facing. It was so long ago
that the duellers now are named sunrise and sunset

and have become part of our days and nights. It's no wonder
we dream the way we do, waking with the taste of another

season in our mouths. And this is a duel fought daily.
Margaret Laurence spent days in a lawn chair

with a wooden bird caller, blowing into it and watching. Listening.
Part of her longed for a story, part of her longed for birds

and another part of her longed for a drink. There was a great lake
between her longing and her having, a river she stood by

and imagined complicated plots involving a hard love and endless
loss. Or Bohemian waxwings and purple martins with epic poems

for clouds written in their lazy landing scrawl. A tall glass of some sort
of elixir that could swoop down from her needled, branching thoughts

and somehow feather herself from herself. Longing saddles
our heart like a horse and rides it to the ground. My daughter took

three days to read the book she was reading. We turned off the Tran-Canada
and headed east. Look for eagles, I told her, but no, she was looking

for a happy ending. She was pinned to the page, tricked
into letting her heart read and now, in the wilderness of story,

in the high trees of the last chapters, word by word she watched
her favourite character die. I've done a lot of research. I know about longing.

It was born over a threshold, neither within nor without. It apprenticed
with *passion*, *desire* and *impatience* and then went abroad to study

with *ache*. All of longing's biographers have gone mad
trying to track what is constantly on the prowl. Longing

never rests, never settles into past tense. I've had to
be careful, watching it in small doses and then studying,

mining the hard rock of these days for hope. Now Robyn's reading
The Diary of Anne Frank. Her heart still so eager. And, being her mother,

I'll continue to point out the eagles, the startled deer in the meadow
on the side of the road. And she will cry; book by book, she will get to know

the world as we all come to see it, the last pull of silver light
like a condor with some great prehistoric wingspan carrying away

the secret that could save us. I still stop what I'm doing to look up,
watch it go and try to figure out where I am in the dark

by the constellations it leaves behind for us like clues.

First Attempt

I love the way we bend down and pick up all the pieces
we've dropped. How we gather the springs and gaskets,

the cogged words of regret and dump them on the kitchen table,
scratch our heads and start again. There's a heroism

in trying, in retracing our steps and turning left this time, instead of right,
that never gets a banquet. Close your eyes and imagine

the lit candles and platters of food, imagine the trophy
in the middle of the table, imagine the speeches. This

is for you. How could you have known anything about
love? You watched your heart walk tentatively down

the driveway of your days, watched it look both ways
and then watched it leave. How could you have known

that words aren't waterproof until it really rained? The seams
of what you said letting in what you really meant

and keeping you up all night. Give anything enough time
and it will somehow fail you. There must be some mathematical equation

to prove this, some cellular division theory, a final paragraph
in a long ago almanac. Tires were made to go flat,

hearts are akin to heirloom plates, to windows
and rocks, to eggs. You'd think that would stop us,

you'd think we'd become a population known for staying
in bed: *why bother, we're just going to die anyway.*

I love that we get up everyday, even when the radio announces
wind chill or flooding. We're all so big and tall and clumsy,

but watch us carry over our small apologies, tending them
like birds fallen from their nests, watch how we hold them

so gingerly in our hands, step slowly to each other
and then offer them up, *I'm sorry, I'm sorry,* the whole flock of hope,

sky and remembered flight right there in our eyes.

Second Attempt

A small boy once planned to empty the Atlantic
with his red pail. Failure, it's been anciently said,
is opportunity. And there he was, no more than ten,

before the entire ocean, determined and sturdy, dipping his pail
and flinging the water out behind him. And at first the ocean
complied with a ballad of low tide but then, slowly, the glissando

of high tide, operatic and demanding. He soon tired
and gave up. The crab-legged moonlight
creeping up to him scurried back and left him dark.

It took him a few days to realize he moved now like a fish,
that he bent around corners and easily glided through thick reeds
of people. *You have a rhythm to you*, his mother marvelled,

combing his hair, *you come and go so easily*. And he did, he grew
and women began falling in love with him. He knew, they said,
how to hold them, to make them feel like full moons and secret, cloistered pearls.

He made the ocean his life study, researching the slow migration
of tortoise, following the underwater path of mollusc. He learned how
fish changed colour by impulses received through their eyes,

and he experimented with corals, long green seaweed, patiently moving fish
from tank to tank, watching in wonder how quickly they adapted.
On his fiftieth birthday, he solemnly drank a glass of wine and returned to the beach

where he had first learned intent, how narrow it was then: a flashlight
and a hallway, he thought, and a hunger, always a hunger.
And though he had studied the ebb and flow of tidal life,

nothing had prepared him for the fish he saw in the inlet
of his youth, descendants of fish he had sat among,
each of them coloured now the iridescent shimmer of secrets

he had whispered. Schools of his long ago yearnings, gilled and finned,
swam around his feet, and he was briefly that boy again,
facing the entire Atlantic, an ocean he could empty himself.

Third

What I meant to do was honour you but you know words.
They're like ants at a picnic, always leaving in a strand of army
for something sweeter. The night I slept where three streams

meet, Elvis's barber spoke to me in a dream. He told me
he wasn't with the early Elvis but was hired right before
the gospel album was released. He had come to tell me

about holiness, how cutting Elvis's hair was like a long
prayer. First he had to put his hand through the halo
and that felt like warm dishwater. I'm still not sure what it all means.

The next night I sat beside a fire fuelled by three times three men
who gathered the wood from nine sacred trees. We spoke of tragedy
to a young boy who pshawed us. *If you're alive*, he told us after we had tried

to convince him we knew what we were talking about, *if you're alive
then that's no tragedy.* Instead of arguing Aristotle, we decided to drink
to the boy's health and soon were in our cups. Only afterwards,

in a cab driven by a former aviator, did I think how great that boy will grow

to be and, in his honour, said the small house prayer I learned
from the architects I know: *May all your chairs face south, may your front door*

open to the east and the rising sun find each window clear. The aviator,
caught in the mood, yelled his final flight prayer to me when we got to the airport.
May you be safer than in god's pocket, he said, and I thanked him,

though god's pocket could be an entire poem
on its own: loose change and its currency: a villanelle of silver coins
and planetary movement. From the air that day, the St. John River was a muscle

of water, striated and flexing like biceps, a deltoid; it bullied the province
of New Brunswick, the scrub and trees of the shore just letting it.
What I meant to do was honour you, your humanness, the way you tie

your newspapers up with leftover string you've saved, the way you think
of ducks when you see crusts, the fillet of sandwich eaten. We are the species
that washes our empty soup cans and tells our children

to fill them with water, freeze them and then take a hammer and nail
and pound holes in the can to make designs of their own: flowers, a cat,
clouds. Then let the ice melt, we tell them, and we tolerate

the dripping cans they leave on the counter, compliment them
on the shapes they've made with the hammer. Then we tell them
wait until after supper, when it gets dark and we put a tea light

in the tin and light it. We are the families sitting around
recycled soup cans magically transformed into lanterns,
constellations of flowers or lopsided cats projected

onto our walls. We have children who use hammers
to pound at tin and ice; studies of fierce intent.
What I meant to do was honour you but you don't need me for that.

Every evening you slide your plates, your forks and knives
and then your hands into what halos feel like. Watch yourselves then,
that impeccable moment of gratitude, the closing of your eyes: blissful.

Refine

At night, with the harbour behind it, the oil refinery
is a great beast turned inside out, its steel

bones, skeletal rivets like joints and its lights, neurons,
nerve cells sparking to the dark. Always there's the question of flame:

heart or brain. I say heart, everyone else in the car
says brain. The true flame of the word is to make pure,

to polish. Here, by day, the true flame is Irving. We need
brand new gods and the mythology of their beginnings.

Someone like Charlie Parker, whose life was too tragic for any studio
to want to make a movie of. He died with his wedding ring,

two horns in the pawn shop. The Lower East Side
of tragedy, bebop staffed on trestles of rush hour

trains. Someone threw a brick through the window of that man's heart
and out flew a bird. It has nothing to do with documentary:

8th Avenue, Bellevue breakdown, rickety tracks across a continent
of addiction. It's how he talked back to it all, sassed a soundtrack no one

can pin down. *What he did*, they'd say and then shake their heads.
Dizzie, trying to explain, just kept putting his fingers together

like a net or a nest trying to catch the essence of one belonging
to the great order of the species *in spite of*. Is it myth because I say so?

This beginning with a man who saw heart in the burning of himself,
who breathed in his own smoke and then played it like raw sugar, crude oil,

the long minute of midnight, being born.

Inspire

O'Keeffe left colour the way you'd leave a lover,
her back to it, refusing. Then the insistence of blue.

Dissect any secret and remove its bone. There is a femur
in silence. Resolve, the long leg of the unspoken beginning to walk.

We will start a new religion. The calla is both pope
and vatican. The time to kneel is now, pray always for rain.

A woman can be part desert and still conquer her thirst.
Her window is a canvas she pulls the curtains over nightly.

Study the technique of cat, the impression it wants to give of nest
and how birds are tricked only once. Know that you share the same weakness.

One chair for solitude, two for friendship. Pickerel, pickerel
and the birth of new colours. Pond, for instance. Reeds.

Anticipate the drive to the mailbox, compose then your letters
of regret. *I'm sorry* is a blank canvas begging for profiles.

We will need a collective noun for all our mothers and the way
they get up to answer the door. We will need a word to murmur when they leave.

Know that love sometimes robs you, its pockets bulging with tubes of paint.
You will be left without colour again and again. You will ask for it.

No more heartbreak. Enough of the same tired line of horizon
tracing rock and root, emblems of him and his goodbye.

Leave the keys in the car for a quick getaway. It's a lot like holding up
a bank, this art. There will be a reward posted, they'll want you dead or alive.

It's tandem. And at first, scorned. There is a tall tree that defines solitude
at the edge of town. Beloved, you are part sky and even more necessary than flame.

The collective noun of our mothers will pass on the name of our species,
the entries of us will describe a plumage, a migration, the letters of regret

we've recycled for their paper and then for their trees.

Apology

The stars fell nightly. At first I'd exclaim and ask her
if she saw that one but too often she'd missed it. So I stopped.

There's a way of keeping your eyes open, of watching wide
so you don't miss anything. She tried. It must take practice, she figured.

It does. And it's tricky. Under a night of meteor showers, the long arc
of awe somehow defines universe in a way that you'd be willing

to get up from the lawn chair, drop the sleeping bag to the ground
and do anything for it, anything. It's easy to keep your eyes open,

it's an essential duty, but the act of watching widely is an all-
or-nothing affair and she's still such a young cluster of girl to see

everything. She watched me pack the old suitcase, watched me write
instructions for Ryan to manage the house, she turned in the front seat

and watched us leave alone. She could be the ambassador
for all small animals. One of her walls is plastered with pictures

of monkeys. All she says after my long rant about the dog,
the sleeping-eat-anything-it-can-find-and-then-puke pet of ours,

is that she loves it. *I love the dog*, she says, *it keeps me company
when you're not home.* O the wide watching of love. Galactic watching

that isn't blind to the pissing on the rug. For a week, she watched stars
falling and I watched her falling into the slow orbit of seeing everything

she's inherited, the heirlooms of clear-cut, of endangered. On the way home,
driving the smudged roads across the island, she announced,

in the dark, in our caravan of car packed to the windows with sand pails
and towels, *the moon isn't following us, it's just always there.*

Vigil

The last river nymph is dying of thirst. She is surrounded
by farmers and can only swallow the lake a teaspoon at a time.

One of the farmers plays a drum quietly for her,
the way he's heard rain on his roof. Another brings his guitar.

The sixth string, he explains, is the earth, the deep bass
of elegy that reverberates into morning like a mirage.

Another farmer lights five candles and places them high above
her bed. *Hyades*, he says, the rising stars that mark the beginning

of the season of rain. One farmer has fallen in love with her
and has lost everything to stay by her side. *Les poissons*,

les poissons is just one of the songs he's composed in her honour.
He whispers small poems about water striders and lily pads,

and in the moments when his shyness ebbs, he kisses her,
thinking *delta*, thinking *cove*, *creek*, *lagoon*.

She has asked for smooth stones to hold, she has asked for reeds,
she sometimes forgets where she is and speaks pickerel,

speaks trout, and they stand around her like she's still a pond
and nod like they understand. One has named his first born

after her. *Naiad*, he announced to his wife, to the midwife,
and plunged the baby into a basin of water. They have gathered

all the coin they can spare and have sent one of their daughters
to a far-away school to learn the art of describing the different movements

of water and eagerly wait her return to teach them rivulet,
teach them current. They tell the nymph all of this,

wishing their words into ladles she can use to dip
and drink from, and are deeply saddened when she begins to resemble

a drying well. She has a gift for each of them, she manages to say,
and when they lean forward, her last breaths are those of a stream,

roiling and rushing at root and rock. Only after she departs
do they realize how refreshed they feel, how quenched.

Restoration

The Mona Lisa on a stretcher, hidden
in an ambulance racing for a safe border mid-war. What

would you save if you just had five minutes in your house?
Think. That dog-eared photograph that caught your daughter

in her bathing suit, cowboy boots and hat when she was three,
offering a teacup full of water to the camera? The book of poems

that still divides the flock of your heart into birds,
and then, even finer, into feathers? Or would you take the five minutes

to just sit in the middle of your living room; *oh my god*,
oh my god, the only mantra you can think of, part gratitude,

part despair? Would you clutch what you've chosen
to your chest or let one hand touch everything as you leave,

the slow caress of farewell you'll breathe,
mouth to mouth in the nights to come?

The curator chose to ride with the painting. I imagine him
sitting by her, hand on her wrapped shoulder, the way he'd sit

with a wife. *I'm right here, it's going to be okay.*
Do we really need to take anything? Every night I sit with my son

and listen to what he's learned in biology. The mystery
of cell division and photosynthesis has coaxed a lush green enthusiasm

around him, creating more oxygen for this house than a tree.
The ambulance was airtight to protect the painting and, by the time it arrived,

the curator had passed out, with his hand still touching her:
a couple in bed after an ordinary day, soft nuzzle of sleep grazing

their conversation. Think how plants slowly exhaled and managed to change
the entire atmosphere of this planet, think of a sixteen-year-old boy

so related to green, he practically blends in, and the curator
waking up beside his Mona Lisa in new surroundings, safe,

and finally breathing the deep treed breath of relief.

Wind Chill and the Absence of Trees in Mexico

O, they'll insulate the moss, the lichen,
even the pale first flowers with their death,

but they're monarch butterflies not oak leaves, their wings
the wordless stationery we write all our letters

of love on. Beloved, they fly from here
to there, an endless hymn to the improbable.

The serious boy from the village must be sent for.
Only he, with his reed flute, can properly mourn

what has happened. There will be a three-day procession
for all those who have followed the butterfly's example

and cocooned themselves in their early states
of despair, who have stayed up late to sweep the floor

and lingered by the open window, bargaining
a decade of their lives for some sort of flutter,

a leaving for a new beginning. There will be a special pew
reserved for the small children who visited the Montreal Botanical Gardens

in 1999, on the verge of a new century, hanging on the last cliff
of the year, entered that rainforest and gave themselves up to it,

transparent with joy. A special seat always for those who allow
their hearts to be seen. The woman, who as a child shared her cup

of water with the tree that gave her shade, will sing a soothing song
to the boy who ran in fright from the butterflies. And he, in turn,

will become ambassador for them, understanding now their accents
and descents. He will announce that the proper mourning period

is a season of planting new trees to replace the clear-cut. Bending,
planting and straightening are all ancient postures for seeking

forgiveness. There will be a moment of silence when all heads
must turn in the direction of each compass point. *Neighbour,*

we must say out loud and mean it.

October, an Elegy

The whole month of October
is an elegy, a used bookstore
getting rained on. This weather
makes me read endings first. Partings
and farewells, the way we're baffled, startled
when happiness falls. Let me tell you about darkness, though,
because there's been enough about light. But first
about the handwritten poem copied out in the back
of a Rilke translation. It begins with *beloved*,
I'm tempted to tell you, or with *rest*,
and is written in the kind of couplets that are made
for each other, lines with stories of how they first met,
and I'm tempted to say that after I read it, light didn't matter,
nor darkness, that poetry somehow gathers
them both into one word. O, how often we are baffled,
startled by our own happiness. I read the poem
and kept its last three unresolved lines: *our*
line break *hearts*. There is a pause always around the word
heart, the history
of leaving, the small right-angled scars of loss. Another line break
then *into*, a space, then the words: *like small trees*. We are made up

of small trees, limbs that reach for each other, forest
of longing, root system of light, small blossoms of darkness
and there is a poem handwritten after pages of Rilke and, after Rilke,
how can our hearts be anything but small trees. The book was used. The lines
unresolved. It was raining so I sat in the store and read
the ending first. Here happiness falls, sometimes
the only difference between *our*
and *hearts* is a line break after a long elegy. This is the season that begins
by ending. The space between light
and darkness is unresolved
as the space between our hearts
and small trees. *Beloved, rest.* It's true, I read the ending first
but I kept reading it until I got all the way back
to the beginning.

After a Line by Hernández

How can we sleep when we love this much? Our beds,
those slim corridors of dream and regret, can barely
contain us. And our hearts, butterflies with insomnia,
fly south, fly back north, fly in every direction to land

finally in the gentle tropic of *yes,* of *I do too.* O, we know
nectar when we see it; we lean forward, we nod,
we touch. *Hmm hmm,* we purr, the motor of us switching
into the gear that will take us off the road and back into

the woods. And the trees, their wolf-whistle when we walk by,
holding themselves open like that, nonchalantly to the sky
when we look back. How can we sleep in these cities, surrounded

as we are by birch, by maples, the instructional guides
to how easy it can be: branch, sky, leaning back
into each other, so simple it can't even be named trust.

Hope

The field notes say these are the times of long
bamboo and chainsaws. The trees, the trees

when they first saw the axe whispered: *it's all right,
the handle is one of us.* There are rumours

that hope wrote its last will and testament in the heart
of a certain environmental physicist. Watch him

interviewed. *Light*, he says buoyantly, *is all we need
to purify the drinking water of the world. Think*, he urges,

looking deep into the camera, *just think why things aren't
working.* He makes science sound like a waltz, a slow dance

cheek to cheek, the hot hand of discovery on the lower back
of the planet. *Nikolai, Nikolai, I beg you*, Tolstoy wrote to his brother

in some sort of fraternal code in every one of his novels,
tell me where you planted your green stick, tell me the secret

of universal happiness. Nikolai buried that stick, dug a hole deep
into midnight, got down on his knees and handed his soul up to the devil

to be tuned in the secret key of no secret. He'd only talk
to small crowds after that, turn his chair to the wall so his voice

would echo and sound like two men. Imagine Tolstoy outside
in his nightshirt, the lantern precariously perched

on the third rewrite of *Anna Karenina*. He had to know,
he thought, digging, the dirt jamming under his fingernails, his knees

muddy. If he had found what his brother long ago buried, the secret hope,
Anna would have sat down on the train, looked up and smiled.

She would have read the note from Vronsky, folded it into her bag
and then left, walking past the train towards home,

where she'd have slowly aged in the tall windows of her time, watching
her children chase the dog around the tree. She'd light more candles,

ring for the maid and ask for another cup of tea. *No*, she'd say,
bring me the whole pot.

We'll need six nails and three pieces of wire, two empty glass
bottles and a hammer. Walk to the east side of the house

and hammer in three nails at eye level, ellipsis, now three more
at ankle height. String each piece of wire vertically from nail

to nail. Tighten the wires by sliding one of the bottles between them
and the house. Use the other bottle as a slide. *You know she's going to*

leave, you know he's going to leave. You know one quiet day we're all going to
leave. Come on in my kitchen, 'cause it's going to be raining outdoors.

It takes practice to play the blues for a whole planet.
A forty-ouncer of loss, acres and acres of whisky straight up and a long story

finally explaining why. Every one of our houses is hungover
from too much family, acoustic and wired, playing on the side

of the streets, noising the low moan of weather, shingles slapping, the cat inside
sleeping, its claws thin as fish bones digging into the chair. When it dreams,

it dreams of schools of fish whispering: *it's okay, the claws are one of us*.
It'll be something simple that sinks us: a small breeze whipping itself

into a frenzy. A tempest. *It's okay*, we'll think, nailing the shutters closed,
it breathes like we do.

Or maybe what we need is a guide who's willing to get wet,
who'll keep her eyes open and let the water line divide her sight

equally into sky and pond. She'll know what happened
to the young boy who ran away from home at fourteen to play

the drums in the *Théâtre Lyrique* for two pounds, fifteen a month.
She'll know the real story and what animal it was that whispered

into his ear nightly for a week before he left, how it begged him
to play the panic beat of its heart, the herd of hunters on its trail.

O, we'll follow her everywhere, leave our jobs for the real thing.
We'll send postcards home. *We're making*, we'll write, *a big difference.*

This is, after all, the crossroads of the last true forest
and there's only a coyote pack of time left patrolling

hungrily along its edge. Look, she'll say, pointing to a tree top,
the sun intent and burning us blind, and we will, just missing

what we were supposed to see, that rare, nearly extinct
feathered thing. But we'll believe her. *Yes*, we'll say, *we saw it.*

We almost saw it.

Tangled

The rose hips are one long moan
of red along the trail. I give you up
every day. And then every day
I walk. Nothing

helps. Crows were hatched from the word
silhouette. You from the word light.
But I promised I wouldn't write about light
any more. You are the opposite

of dark. You are the moving water on the wall
when leaves are dappled and I need the surface
of a river to remind me where I started from.
Call me home the way you do. There is something

about the tamaracks I want to tell you about.
Nothing to do with the way the sun moves
through them, its long leaving touching each yellowed
needle, nothing about the slouched shoulders

of them. Not tamaracks but, for here, larches,

trees that are convinced all summer
they are coniferous then look around in November, bewildered
by how bare they've become. I won't write of it,

I'll write around it. There is a great darkness
at the foot of bewilderment. There is a month
of Sundays needing something holy. I never thought
it would be me kneeling like this. I give you up

every day and every day I yearn to write of what I promised
I wouldn't. It's a way of holding out
long blades of sweet grass between fence slats. The hungry animals
that graze our hands are shy at first, their tongues hot. I give you up

because I think I can. At the end of the long moan,
the rose hips whisper flower. I've confused memory
with reverence. What is not dark, the opposite, the reach of it
warms my face. I give you up and then try to find you again.

But you've never left. You bring the unmentionable
out in me. Love is a larch. It stands in a forest,
trying to blend in, and is surprised by its shape
when it's finally bared. It is November and I am stripped

of you. It's for the best. There is a river splitting the trees in two.
I started by wanting to cross it. You called me home
and a silhouette of crows stuttered across the sky.
There are hungry animals and a long moan of hips,

darkness, darkness and I am shy and on my knees. There is something
about giving up and you that always goes together,
and that is somehow holy. You know what I can't say
because I promised not to. It rhymes with sight

and with right. Your touch is home and gives me up
to bewilderment in this first month of darkness.
I moan a red flower along your hips on the trail
of fallen silhouettes. The crows are a mystery

and all that is holy. See how love has bared its branches for us
in its red season without flower. And in spite of the cold
there will be a blooming of hot tongues,
and melting thorns. An animal is hatching

in your long moan. I won't say holy. My hand is held out,
grazing on your hunger. I'm pressed hard here against the fence
of all I've left unspoken.

Beginning with a Line by Nuala O'Faolain

I've hurt myself in my life, I thought, by leaving
a thousand beautiful places. And never taken the time
to leave them properly as beautiful places

require leaving. If I could press my lips
to your hip again and taste distance
in your skin, teach my tongue

to be fluent in a language that will persist
until all our secret words return to roost in this heart.
The lone silhouette of desire, its wings outstretched

in the sky above the dunes, a heron who translates
into again and again or *return*. If I could go back
to the thousand places and lay my hands on each of them,

the knobby bedspread of the night before, the thick-leafed tree
of the garden, I would. I would. And then, properly this time,
with reverence, with meaning, I would bend to each of them

and place my lips upon them as if they were you, as if they were
you.

A Week

mornings

Each hour takes a turn sitting in your kitchen chair. *I'm hungry*, it keeps saying, minutes apart.

Some mornings break the furniture. This bed is too small, this love too hot.

Birds fly hard at pulling up the light like turnip, potatoes, the root of a young poet.

The subspecies of chance are small flocks of mornings. They halo the feet of your days with whisper: *Come on.*

Your nightclothes are all sleeves: hold me; don't leave yet; come back.

The way you press your lips to your hand and still taste him, the moon faint in the sky.

East of morning is a mine shaft into the dream of a stranger who won't let go of your gold.

evenings

The last light, too small for the front, drives its ambulance and picks up the wounded.

Winter nights are overweight watchmen, grumpy at being awake. There are surveillance cameras in the hallways of your sleep.

The village women, holding the town clock hostage, are demanding more nocturnal men.

A tanker carrying lullabies has flipped on highway 101. A convoy of alarm clocks is being shipped in. *It's awful,* an official has said. *We must wake everyone up.*

We need three miles to unroll the map of the continent Night. It's not drawn to scale. The dream you had about being lost is this acre here, by the woods.

Loneliness is evening's natural resource. Entire lifetimes have been spent drilling offshore of memory.

"Marry me," evening, down on its knee, begs dawn. And dawn, with a little secret of its own, agrees.

New Year's Eve 2001

There is not much left to say. The teenagers I hurry by
in the dark are now our sons. The Christmas tree thrown
on the fire at midnight erupted into the new year, a constellation of embers
just below Orion's belt and the moon. Some of us couldn't even think
of something to wish for. It's been like that. We've been left
speechless. Late December and now early January. The year behind us,
a skulking gang of memories waiting for us to slow down,
to slip. Our sons calling out to us from the trees. It's me, one of them yells
when I pass by, walking, as I've been told to, as if I have a purpose.
But he knows that I don't. He sees me sitting,
looking out at the sky when I should be making supper,
waiting for that moment when it becomes dark.
There is no purpose to this except to see it coming,
which I never do. He's outside, I'm heading in,
even the dog has aged. It's subtle, the long-legged pines
are swallowed up first, the shed disappears. In dreams
I'm still bending over him, helping him draw.
The houses on the hill step back from their porch lights,
cars turn into headlights, bus stops to street lights.
He's hungry, he says and I get up, switch on the lights.
He eats, then goes back out. There are keys to this house

hidden outside. I can't stay awake long enough anymore to let him
back in. Somebody wished for money, someone said good health.
I hardly knew them. *Here are question and reply*, I wanted to say
more to the night than to any of them. *And the fire*
reflected in the thinking eye. So subtle
and with smooth machinery, eventually even the night steps back,
turns into a pale, last star with all we're left of it slowly burning out.

Lawn

I spent last summer imagining how love should have been
and nagging my son to mow the lawn.

Now, covered in the early snow of January,
the uncut grass, the sepia blooms of long dead weeds

are actually beautiful. All the other lawns are uniformly covered,
ours looks like Canadian art, something you'd see

on a greeting card, a blank greeting card for those occasions
that don't fit the standard wish. Like this one:

Dear Ryan, If someone had shown me a photograph
of the long grass, the wheat of the lawn in snow,

if I had known how beauty would distract me, keep me at the window
to marvel at the colour brown, I would've let you sleep

those August mornings. It wasn't a summer of letting go;
we had all let go by then. It was a summer of having been left

by the grand idea of who we thought we were. Of course you needed
to sleep. It took a season, the one season where everything falls

to the ground, for me to realize it had nothing to do with the lawn
or garbage day but with the way the heart can shut down

and how alone we sometimes are together. It was an overgrown summer,
your nights crowding into my mornings. And now, in the beginning

of winter, it's the light I watch stretching, the blossom of it against the dark.
We're perennial, Ry, and we only need such a small space, winter, the briefest of light,

 to keep growing.

Patience

Don't give it to us in metric. We need gallons
of it, a mile in your shoes, quarts of the sweet elixir
of calmness, serenity to coat these burrs

of rebuttal stuck in our throats. The instruction
guide to the universe is pages and pages long,
in all languages, the same word: *breathe,*

respirer, atmen. That's all. *C'mon, c'mon, c'mon* isn't an incantation
first scratched on papyrus in the ancient times
of hurry. It doesn't magically put its fingers on the big

clock and wind it any faster. The days are made
of molecule-moments, each with its own
special destiny and black box. You didn't imagine a time

difference between you and your teenage son.
His minute is not a molecule but an epoch
filled with the great disaster of dog waiting

to be taken out, the jungle of lawn growing through

window, the ellipsis of busy signal as he discusses
various ways to make a ton of cash without doing

anything. Remember the first and only step
in life's little handbook, that gentle urge to breathe.
Each breath, after all, is worth more than its weight

in gold. Think of the currency of a long pull of air
into our lungs, the bouquet of bronchia blossoming
in our chests and where we'd be without it.

I wish I could tell you about some guy, call him the legendary Bob,
and how, with the power of pure will, he made the old man
in front of him drive faster. I wish I could tell you he could clear

grocery aisles of meandering women but I'd be lying.
Old men drive slow, sometimes with their left signal
blinking like a panting dog hanging out the window.

And they never turn, so don't hold your breath. The women
don't meander, they dream of someone else picking out the Shake
'n Bake, someone saying: *don't get up, I'll make it tonight.*

Breathe. No one ever has just 8 items in the express lane
and who carries exact change? You'll bend and pick up
wet towels daily, imagine it as a metaphor for telling time.

Soon the hour of dry, folded towels, the hour of the empty
house will chime. *Respirar.* And in the silence, your heart,
there are the hands of many memories working. Time

is the gasket, the thin slice of hope that fits between
the pieces. Here it works its quietest skill of undoing,

of slowly sorting what to keep
and who to let go.

Backwards, or, Returning

Think of a country and western song played
backwards, the pick-up truck pulling a U-turn

in old man Smith's yard and rattling on back
home. Think of missing the familiar thump of tail, the way

the leash still haunts the hook by the door and then
listen for the bark in the driveway. Think of your heart

being mended, the afternoon an eruption of buttercups
and long plowed hours, the acreage of your back, the slow

rain of tongue. Play this backwards. Our dead
are in the dining room, waiting to be fed. You finally fixed

the gate to the field so we know that our days are
corralled, a herd of them grazing, their gentle eyes

patient with our unsure hands. And our unsure hands,
fumbling with all we've been given, undoing each other,

the great ocean of beginning calling our bones back
to the water and we sink, O we sink to the floor, your dark hair

eclipsing my breast. Play this backwards and we're speechless,
the blank page reunited with its forest of trees by the quiet stream,

and the light wind it has missed the most, the breeze it longs for,
that it lies down bare for us to write about, stops its mournful search,

the reunion of limb and breath, the shiver of leaves we're all so akin to.

Demystified

A seventh century mystic put a piece of wood
on his fire and watched the flame take it over.

Here is a lesson on giving, he wrote by its light.
And was about to write more, write the whole

lesson in the form of a tree but something stopped him.
A vision, maybe, in the flames, or the way his potato

was cut in two, the bigger half an island north
on his almost empty plate. Here is a lesson

on hunger, he thought, gathering his writing tools,
his only other garment. And left his plate of potato,

left his fire, his lesson on giving, to learn more about leaving.

For seven days and seven nights I prayed exclusively
to him. I prayed for him to return to his hut and sit back down,

to cut his potato in four and point to the pieces and say:
this is your heart, it has four sections. This section holds

the lesson of leaving. He came once in a dream, nodded,
put his fork into my heart, cut it in four pieces and

ate it. Then he asked for an onion. Onions, he told me,
make him cry and my heart so filled with tears is hurting

his eyes.

He spent several days by a stream sketching various devices
to raise water. *Noria*, he wrote later, beside his drawing

of a bucket. There is a whole page devoted to pulleys
next to a page with a small poem written on it. *Leaving*,

it begins, and the rest of it is blurred by the stream splashing
onto the page. I fill the sink with cold water and take down

a glass. Somehow, I think, pouring water must be
a lesson. I pour until the glass is half full and stand it upright

in the sink. A domino of decades is set into backward motion
and I can almost see him leap to his feet and excitedly dip his hat

into the rushing clear water and then drink from it like a cup.

Last night it seemed the stars were falling, he wrote
on the next page, *and tonight I was afraid the night sky*

would be empty. When he stopped writing he looked straight up
at me. *Go outside*, he said, *and see what you've been missing*.

I can hear him breathe behind me when he points past the street light.
That is the ancient constellation *Noria*, he tells me. Dipper, I suppose.

We must get to work or your heart will soon flood.

He sends me a message the next day in the form of a poem
about onions: *Lark of my house, laugh often.* He places the book

in my hand and then prepares to sleep. The stable he's using
is filled with horses. *Give me your boots*, he says, before lying down,

and I hand him the tired shoes I've worn through all of this.
He puts them in the stirrups backwards and then slaps the rump

of the darkest horse. The night is like flame and we watch
the horse give in to it like wood. *There you go*, he tells me,

there goes the ghost of you. Leaving has left.

Notes

"His Green Age" is a line by Dylan Thomas. The list of the words Thomas used most were found in *The World of Dylan Thomas* by Clark Emery.

The photograph of Ellen Terry is credited to Window and Grove, London. The title, "Here Lies the Water and Here Stands the Man" is a line from *Hamlet*. The italicized quotes are lines from that play as well.

"Kindred" is for Helen Humphreys.

"Refine" was written after the movie *Bird Now*, directed by Marc Huraux.

"After a Line by Hernández". From a poem by Miguel Hernández, translated by Timothy Baland, "28 [Death, enclosed in a bull's hide]".
> "Like you, I can't sleep, because I love
> too many things, and my heart, dressed
> like the dead, overflows toward the universe."

"Beginning with a Line by Nuala O'Faolain" opens with a sentence from her novel, *My Dream Of You*.

The italicized lines in "New Year's Eve 2001" are from "Winter Night," a poem by Edna St. Vincent Millay.

In "Demystified," *Lark of my house, laugh often* is from the Miguel Hernández's poem "Lullaby of the Onion".

Acknowledgements

Thanks to the editors of *The Antigonish Review*, *The Malahat Review* and *Canadian Literature* where some of these poems first appeared.

Thanks to The Canada Council and The Nova Scotia Arts Council for support while writing this book. And thanks to Monika and Jane at The Writers' Federation of Nova Scotia for the most welcoming space a writer could find.

With much gratitude to everyone at Brick Books. Kitty Lewis, Maureen Harris and especially my editor, Stan Dragland, for his ears, his eyes and O, his finely-tuned heart.

For their conversation, their laughter, their willingness to karaoke, to dance, to break out in a sweat, my love goes to: Debbie and Kevin, Peggy, Grant and Virginia, Genevieve and Pam.

For keeping me lit: Joanne, Jane, Darren, Lynn, Lori and Gayle.

For convincing me to sit at my desk when I could barely get out of bed, for phoning every day and letting it ring until I answered, for keeping poetry resuscitated, for listening to Lucinda and drinking beer with me long distance, Helen: you give a lovely light.

A chirp and a car alarm right back to the Northern Mockingbird who kept me company with the lounge act of impressions that it rehearsed early, early every morning outside my bedroom window.

A hawk right over the truck, always, for Peter.

S ue Goyette lives in Halifax, Nova Scotia with her family. Her first collection of poetry, *The True Names Of Birds* (Brick Books, 1998) was short-listed for The Gerald Lampert, The Pat Lowther and The Governor General's Awards for Poetry. Her novel, *Lures* (HarperCollins Canada, 2002) was short-listed for The Thomas Raddall Award for Fiction. She's been a member of the faculty at The Maritime Writers' Workshop, The Banff Wired Studio, and the Sage Hill Writing Experience. She is currently working on her second novel.